Poetry, Prose & Penguins and Today is Another Great Day

FOURTH EDITION

Written and Illustrated by

CLAUDIA DIANNE STUART

Kendall Hunt
publishing company

Front cover image © Claudia Stuart
Author photo courtesy of Rik Andersen

Kendall Hunt
publishing company

www.kendallhunt.com
Send all inquiries to:
4050 Westmark Drive
Dubuque, IA 52004-1840

ISBN 979-8-7657-0691-6

Published in the United States of America

Contents

II Prose 165

Other Books

My Private Stock
Expressions
All Along Life's Journey
African Americans in Amarillo
Living Out Loud
Sociology—the New Millennium
Sociology—the New Millennium, 2nd Edition
Sociology—Beyond the Millennium, 3rd Edition
Sociology—Beyond the Millennium, 4th Edition
Sociology—Beyond the Millennium, 5th Edition
Sociology—Beyond the Millennium, 6th Edition
Sociology—Beyond the Millennium, 7th Edition
West Texas A&M University and the Devil's Kitchen,
Education Through the Ages
Poetry, Prose and Penguins
Poetry, Prose and Penguins, 2nd Edition
Poetry, Prose and Penguins, 3rd Edition

Foreword

My name is Freda Powell, and I am the first African American woman elected to the Amarillo City Council in 70 years and the first African American woman to serve as Mayor Pro Tem. My best title and the one that I am most proud of is servant leader in the Amarillo community.

The poet Claudia Stuart has been my friend since the early 1980s. She was a probation officer then, and I was a young woman in my 20s. She continues to work throughout the Amarillo community as a tireless advocate, serving others and always ready to take action. I am inspired by her wisdom, professionalism, the way she carries herself as a woman and her spiritual commitment. She is not only a role model for me still today, but also stands as a role model for her daughters and grandchildren. Having served as a consultant to various justice, social and civic groups on issues of law enforcement, probation and parole, the American criminal justice system and cultural diversity, she has credible standing on the issue of racism in America today. In "Don't Fan the Flames of Racism," Claudia expresses the injustice and inequality of the subjugation of African Americans as slaves and in chains since the 17th century.

As I watched the evening news on Memorial Day, I began to lean forward to the edge of my chair as I learned of Mr. George Floyd's death and the way he died. I was heartbroken, frustrated, angry and devastated that police brutality continues to exist. I would not have believed the circumstances surrounding his death if I had not seen the brutal and painful video with my own eyes. Mr. Floyd was helpless on the ground, handcuffed and feeling the pressure of a knee to his neck. Thanks be to God for this video! Because of the inhumane treatment and the lack of action by the three officers who watched, even as Mr. Floyd is calling his deceased mother and then transitioned to be with her. In the writer's mind, she lives in a community where everyone is united and moving together as a human race. She wakes up every day and asks God to use her for the good to make a difference in someone's life. Then, she leaves her home and when she steps out onto "Mean Streets," reality returns. Claudia reminds us that on "Mean Streets," there is no justice and no peace. "Mean Streets" becomes an avenue for one's voice to be heard on behalf of the high-profiled lives that continue to be lost even now in the 21st century. More than ever, we need diversity to unite and move our nation's communities forward together.

In the wake of police brutality and the COVID-19 pandemic, Claudia describes the effects of the virus as it relates to our economy, human consequences and physical and mental well-being. We are all together but separately social distancing, washing our hands, sanitizing, and wearing our masks. We are human beings who need face-to-face interaction and the touch of others.

In the writing of "Lord I See You," Claudia reminds us that when we feel overwhelmed by racism, police brutality, COVID-19, and the challenges of life, turning to our Lord and Savior should be our first response. God is real even now! He is everywhere. We do not have to look up, we just need to look around. Most of the time, He is carrying us. We just need to talk to Him and trust in Him.

> *"Don't Fan the Flames of Racism." What will you, the reader, be inspired to do now to help right a wrong and make a difference in someone's life? "Lord I See You" and I hear You!*

Freda Powell, Former Mayor Pro Tem *Amarillo, Texas*

Preface

Claudia Stuart is a poet, a professor, and a powerful force for good in the world. Her poetry is usually optimistic; a reinforcement of her certainty that Life and God are good even if some people could use some improvement. She will uplift you, inspire you, and if you allow it, make you think. Read these poems slowly. Let them sink in. Pull them around you like a soft blanket and let them keep you warm.

Claudia Stuart is one of those people who comes into your life and makes you better. She is adamant in opposing evil and positive about doing what is right. Her spirit allows you to become adamant and positive right along with her. When she reaches out to you and opens her world to you, the world just becomes a better place to be. She does this through her poetry, too.

Claudia Stuart is passionate about penguins. This obsession began several years ago and shows no signs of abating. Penguins pushed her to grow beyond poetry on paper to poetry in art, making penguin art as beautiful and as thoughtful as her poetry. Her penguins, like her poetry, have a depth that increases the more you ponder them.

Poetry is able to ease into your soul in a way that prose often cannot. Poetry engages your emotions, holds up a mirror so you can see yourself better, and lets you see more clearly, live more deeply. Good poetry speaks to you in ways that words alone cannot describe. It can change you before you know it or bring up defenses you never knew you had.

Reading poetry is almost as much an art form as is writing poetry. You don't just skim the words of one and go on to the next. You read the words, maybe even speak them aloud, and listen to what they have to say. You focus on your own reaction, hear what the words have said to your heart, find that knowing place where Truth lives. You hold that poem for a while, live with it, taste it. Only when you have absorbed all you can for the moment do you set it down gently and rest. Be mindful of the silence before you take on the next poem, for they have power.

In reading *Poetry, Prose and Penguins,* treat each poem, and each penguin, with care. Revel in the love, the joy, and the passion of the author and let her art fill your soul. Your world will be brighter. You will find more love in your heart. You will find a smile on your face, one of deep satisfaction or one of wonder. Bask in the glory of all that is Claudia Stuart and realize that her true gift is to reveal to you that you are glorious, too.

Jean Stuntz

Acknowledgment

I acknowledge God in all things and offer many special words of gratitude to my family, especially Harold, Dietra and Farrah for their support and kind words of encouragement throughout this journey. My inspiration for this work comes from various people, environments and social events occurring around the world. Special thanks to Rik Andersen, Jean Stuntz and Freda Powell for their interest and contribution to the book, I am also grateful for Jenifer Kunz, and Marty Kuhlman, Delores Thompson, Judy Turner, Renee Jones, Michael Stewart, Vernon White, Jr., Barbara Chapman, Randy White and Courtney White in understanding the importance of social commentary and reaching out to build bridges among people in communities. I dedicate this work of poems, axioms and penguins to my grandchildren: Raquelle Lawrence, Christian and Jonathan Shorten, and Langston and Maya Williams who have come to love and appreciate all of my fine, feathered friends. And above all, to my mother, Claudia White, who even in her absence remains a huge source of inspiration especially concerning the importance and need for social justice not only for ourselves, but others as well, for we are indeed our brother's keeper.

PENGUIN ART

By

Claudia Stuart

Part I
Poetry

A Man, a Plan and a Kitchen

The table was bare
Made of solid rock
And generally used
Just for eating.

But, then there was
Once upon a time
That the table was
Used for a meeting.

Many had gathered
Young men and old
Embarking upon a
Huge mission.

To build a college
With ag in mind
And lamenting about
The tuition.

1917 it was
As they all came
From various parts
Of the state.

The governor was there
Ranchers and farmers, too
Businessmen and all
Through the gate.

Hurry we must
With the people's trust
To see this task
Through fruition.

For upon this rock
On this solid ground
In a place called
The Devil's Kitchen.

So, fast forward today
From 100 years hence
We still plan to
Enhance education.

WT is the place
And with God's grace
We'll build with
Great expectation.

Gathering bright minds
Diverse as they come
And all others
Without delay.

We've shuttered the old
Now, on with the new
Build the high-rise in
The sky today.

Our students will learn
From subjects they like
Taught by able-minded
Academicians.

From upon this rock
On this solid ground
In a place called
The Devil's Kitchen.

A Prayer

Dear Lord,

I bow humbly before thee,

thanking you for the many blessings bestowed upon us and praying,

Lord, for forgiveness from all sins.

Dear Lord, we ask that you keep us safe from all hurt, harm, and danger.

I thank you for the opportunities we've had throughout the year,

Dear Lord, and I pray that as you give us a new day and a new year

that we are prepared to enter in and do things, Father God, in a new way.

For if we continue doing things the same old way,

we cannot expect to get new and different and better results.

I pray that we love one another.

Dear Lord, let us be diligent, deliberate, and decisive,

being obedient onto you, that we may resolve the issues we have before us in this town, in cities and states throughout the United States, and around the world at large.

Father God, let us be cooperative, let us be inclusive,

collaborative and determined to work together to resolve the issues facing us so that we may enter thy Kingdom without a spot, without a wrinkle, and without a stain.

Thy will be done. In the name of Jesus, I pray.

Amen.

A Tribute to Charles Warford

A gentle giant as he stood
    With a plan for all to see,
How to make things better
    In his community.

A caring voice, an easy smile
    To get you through each day,
To help encourage many to greatness
    Without the pleas and may.

He saw youth as the brain trust
    From each generation to come,
Preparing them, not sparing them
    For the lifelong run.

He made a life and gave a life
    And will be remembered by some,
For what he did for all he knew
    And the obstacles he'd overcome.

Amarillo

Born out of the prairie
The ancient lure of Indians
Indians and Buffalo
Roaming the High Plains.

Eking out an existence
In a land so free and the
Wilds of the night drawing
Fire and fury and remains.

Call it what you will.
Ragtown, Oneida,
Amarillo, and
The Yellow Way.

All are names
For this great land of
That big sky
And promise.

In the 1880s, settlers came
And staked out a claim
On the land they would
Soon surmise.

Charles Goodnight, and John Adair,
Started the JA Ranch without a care.
Lee Bivins and Ernest Thompson, too
All great pioneers in times so new.

Henry Sanborn, Father of Amarillo,
And Joseph Glidden
Had businesses wherever
They would go, to name a few.

People buying and selling
Across the plains,
Building homes, ranches, and ridges
With great means.

Quanah Parker and Mathew "Bones" Hooks
Came upon the scene,
To round out the culture
Of lives in between.

Out of the dust
The town grew up
And became what
It was meant to be.

A land made of counties,
Potter and Randall,
Around a great canyon
Called Palo Duro, come see.

Buildings and bridges,
Playas, rivers, and roads,
Inns and inventions,
And many stories untold.

The dust bowl, long gone,
Tornadoes took homes.
Rebuilding unyielding with
Communities into the fold.

Industry burst forth
Of cattle, cotton and grain.
Later, oil, gas, and commerce
To explain.

The railroads were seen
Miles and miles to the sky.
Occasionally, a passerby,
Nobody to complain.

Baggage, people, and dreams
With far-reaching means
To cultivate, communicate,
And stimulate.

Moneylenders were lending,
The economy was bending.
People were
Happy to celebrate.

For the schools,
There were plenty,
And children, many,
As young ones grew up in this place.

People thrived to get by
In this land of big sky
With no problems and
No room for debate.

Religions, they flourished,
And people nourished
In this great land
Of the "Bible Belt".

As Sundays came and went,
Children saw their days spent
In the churches, at the altars
Where they knelt.

At the end of the day,
Come what may,
Amarillo is here to stay
On the High Plains.

Energy, there is plenty
Of helium power and wind.
Oh, that pungent smell of money,
Don't complain.

A handshake and a smile
Will last for a while
As values take hold
Of the land.

No matter the season,
For whatever reason,
Diverse people live in this region
Developing their brand.

In the land of the sun
When the day is done
One can reflect on
The days of yore.

And be thankful of dreams
Of rodeo scenes,
And possibilities of
Much, much more.

Wind turbines and urban,
Universities and suburban,
Merchants came from
All over the world.

The Amarillo Air Base grew us,
And others pursued us
To build aircraft with
A tremendous whirl.

Leadership driving.
People still conniving.
Medical center thriving
As the best.

Arts and entertainment,
Buildings of containment,
All dot the landscape
To the west.

What is safe will be revered
As people living without fear
And the city gently growing,
Upon the Panhandle plateau.

Commuters near and far
Will travel in their car
Out Route 66 and the
I-40 corridor.

Lots of points to see.
Cadillac Ranch making history,
The Big Texan staking claims
On steaks to eat.

People friendly all day long,
Will leave you with a song
About Amarillo in "Texas."
Hats off and take a seat.

Apartheid

This is not apartheid in America today, is it?
As we see our children gather round and go outside but cannot play.

Our streets are filled with hatred as people try to separate us by color, cast and creed.

Our voices go unheard and our pain unbridled as we look toward the morning sun and ask, what happened?

This is not apartheid in America today, is it?

When gone are the lunch programs and breakfast programs in our schools to feed our children to keep them healthy with nutrition, nourishment to make them whole.

As we see black and brown hued faces pressed against the windows wondering, is this my America?

I have friends no longer friendly, and I have desires no longer envied by a people who seems losing self-control.

There are cultures no longer singing, and fathers no longer bringing a plan of action to fit the mold.

This is not apartheid in America today, is it?

As I travel to many places on the streets so wide and so vast and come to an end no longer caring and no longer free.

I see the many wonders, bridges, buildings that were built by the sweat of the hands of my people in a land no longer serving the likes of me.

In a country where people pay their taxes and find the role on their back is pain and pressure and frustration with grim rewards at the end of the day.

This really takes me to a place that is all about the race and the pathetic treatment around the way.

Yet, I see in God's grace that I can go to a higher place and feel the comfort and the joy that grows within. I have a Savior who died for me and blessed my spirit and set me free.

It can not stay dark forever because the light shines through the heavens and washes all the tragic pain away.

This is my America built by my people large and small often there to save the day.

Washing, cleaning, cooking, picking, training, weaning and other duties that other people would not do.

Being constantly reminded that we build, and we can mine it and find solace as we strive for equal pay and have a clue.

That with education all about our nation, we were shown a different path that we could take. It was built on many rumors that people could be humored into thinking that we are equal in every way.

We are born with certain freedoms, gifts that we cherish and hold dear and we dare not ever give it all away. For as we vote our passion in a nation that is unyielding, we will strike a chord so everyone can play.

I see a tent that will grow bigger as we roll our sleeves in vigor and walk the streets to register people that will vote.

We will see throughout the nation people joyous without temptation to sit down at any table for which to eat.

There are events that make us stronger with the words that make us hunger for a better life in a better way and greater peace.

Freedom is not free, and it is up to you and me to remember to pass down history of our past. Then, our children will grow up knowing that the things that we are showing is how to tap into the freedoms at our feet.

We are strong and we are humbled, and on our path, we may stumble, but we get up and we stand strong and free.

This is not apartheid in America today, is it?

No, no way, not tomorrow, not today and we will not accept that this could happen in our time.

We will continue being eager to have our voices there to greet you at the table while we will gladly take our seat. And as the pie is sliced and diced and even with a little spice, we share pieces of our daily bread.

This is not apartheid in America today, is it?

No, not today, and not tomorrow.

We stand tall and look up with no fear, no pain, no anger, and no dread.

Art Out Loud Circling the Museum

Water streaming from a babbling brook
Across the High Plains
And Apache bow and arrow carefully
Poised at what it aims.

Oil derricks dotting
The massive landscape.
Union soldiers in uniforms
Preventing escape.

Trunks filled with memorabilia,
Treasures and stuff.
Windmills powering life's energy
Making sure there is enough.

Pottery, china, flasks, guns, glasses,
All kinds of things
Depicting some of the trends, fashion
Designs that they bring.

People meeting people, working with
People, enslaving people.
Others running, hunting, rowing,
Charging to that distant steeple.

Pictures, many pictures
Of life in a world gone by.
Art and books and documents
Explaining the reasons why.

Art on every floor in every
Crevice along the way
Forming culture, ways of living
And cherished memories of the day.

All in the great building
Housing life and art and pain,
Yet, also, the joy of living in the
Past with history reframed.

The voices screaming from the
Gravesites and with words so profound.
Learning about other cultures
You find it written in the ground.

The walls tell a story
So interesting to note.
All about our ancestors,
In history books and quotes.

History is the story
So relatable as it unfolds,
Until you reach the ending and
Lives upended with the holes.

Researching and explaining
Takes expressing and complaining
To understand the truth
Of days gone by.

Hunting and gathering in
Some cultures give way
To industries in others
All for pay.

Then, comes the exploitation
Of persons left without a nation
With meager ways of raising children
Without family, foe, nor kin.

Art out loud covers many genres
Including art, paintings, and collages,
And syncopated music, dance and
Singing too.

The drums are heard
From many places
By ones of different races
Making beautiful harmony for all of us.

The religion of reservations
And regard to anticipation
Of better lives for
People everywhere.

Listen long and listen hard
As they talk about the Lord
And promises of love and peace.
Do we dare?

The oil derricks up to the tip top.
Next week's program on Tik Tok.
Wagons rolling in the background, stop.
Old model T's in the fore ground, locked.

Making the circle go round
And round.
People and cultures
All about the grounds.

Warriors fighting.
Hear the sound of
Soldiers yelling,
Put in another round.

Can you feel the power of the trains?
Can you see the majesty of the plains?
Can you hear the mighty wind as it rings?
Can you smell oil, swine, and cattle in their domain?
Can you hear the many voices sing?
Can you tell what tomorrow will bring?
Can you? Can you?

Then there's quiet
About the land.
All are covered in mud and sand.
What about that other plan?

The next chapter is being played
As forefathers have been laid.
Life goes on and plain to see the
Next few chapters about you and me.

Life goes
  Around
    In circles.

Black Lives Matter A Masterpiece

Black lives matter.
    Damn right we do.
Who do I have to convince of that,
    Me or you?

I see it in the eyes
    As I meet you day after day
In the parks, schools and playgrounds.
    Yes, when we go out to play.

Little children being afraid
    To move ahead and grab the swing.
It's okay to do it.
    It's still a play thing.

Older children trembling
    In the classrooms to compete,
Thinking they lack the power
    To use their minds and think.

Even in the workplace
    When treatment is unfair at best
Shrugging shoulders of complacency,
    I'm done, you do the rest.

So, now our children suffer
    Shot down in cold blood today.
He thought things would be different
    From the times he was at play.

Just walking through the neighborhood
    Puts lives in jeopardy.
Strutting in my hoodie
    Being free to be me.

Where is the threat to your life
    In this big place called the earth?
We came into being the same way
    From the moment of our birth.

I am in the image
    Of God who saves us all.
Yet, we have doubt within ourselves
    To heed the clarion call.

Black lives matter.
    Damn right we do.
Who do I have to convince of that,
    Me or you?

I am a child of God
    Built fresh to stand the test
Of living all together
    And striving for the best.

My work, my toils, my troubles
    Mount each and every day.
Teaching, preaching and reaching
    For that Black child to say. . .

You are a worthy creature
    To be alive today.
Always keep your head up high
    So, Christ can see you stay.

Be strong in your convictions,
    And mighty with your mind
Yes, body, mind and spirit
    No one can be that blind.

Treat others as your brother
    And want the same for them,
With justice and love for humanity
    That sense we got from Him.

Black lives matter.
    Damn right we do.
Through with convincing others,
    Now, it's up to you.

Blessings

Life is such a blessing
    And I thank God
Each and every day

For all that He
    Has given me
As I go along my way.

The rain clouds in
    The morning
The stars in the sky at night

The mountains, hills
    And dales
And the birds in flight

The tiny, little
    Creatures
Scurrying up the path

The waves in all
    Its fury
The surges and the wrath

The insects with
    Their sounds
So small

A child
    Playing with
Their ball

The lives we are allowed
    To touch
Each day

Give us joy
    And
A brighter way

All are
    Blessings
Large and small

And I am
    Thankful
For them all.

CStuart

Breathe

You are fading fast.
Tell me how you feel,
What you need.

Let me do it for you.
Let me get it for you.

Breathe, breathe, breathe.

Let me hold you In my arms.
Let me hold you one last time.
Let me hold you one last.
Let me hold you one.
Let me hold you.
Let me hold.
Let me.
Let. . . .

I can't breathe.
I can't breathe.
I can't breathe.
I can't breathe without you with me.
I can't breathe without you by my side.
I can't breathe without you by.

I can't breathe without you.
I can't breathe without.
I can't breathe.
I can't.
I. . . .

Come to Me Softly

Come to me softly
    In the night
Gently holding me
    Oh, so tight.

Come to me softly
    In the night
Stroking me with
    All your might.

Come to me softly
    In the night
Feeling me making
    It right.

Come to me softly
    In the night
Strongly caressing me
    That's nice.

COVID-15

Just a little bit more, please.

COVID-19

This is my arm outstretched halfway to you,
For you
Around you
By you
With you
Toward you
Me and you.

Creative Writing
A Must Do

I enjoy breathing

I enjoy walking

I enjoy running

I enjoy dancing

I enjoy singing

Something I truly enjoy like the air that I breathe is creative writing.

Hence, creative writing is something I must do!

So, how do we get started?

It begins with a creative thought.

Let your minds wander—over fields and valleys
the motions of the oceans
the vastness of the sky
the plains and high plains
the hot and torrid Serengeti
the earth and her inhabitants

Now, we begin to focus on the thoughts and think of the words to express your feelings about the thoughts. Use guided imagery to gather the words into sentences on a page making sense out of images and thoughts into words. Write enough sentences on the page to become chapters. Write enough chapters to become a book and hold on to more thoughts, and more words and more pages and more chapters to become more books and on and on and on.

This is my focus for today.

Creative writing—a must do.

Don't Call Me a Refugee I Am An American

Yesterday, I was proud to be living in this land
    Yesterday, I was housed on a street on either hand
Yesterday, I was fed by the living tree of life
    Yesterday, I was with family and comforted without strife.

Today, I have a different truth that hit me in the face
    Today, I have no food to eat nor water to run this race
Today, I have no money to put shoes upon my feet
    Today, many strangers are all that I meet.

Tomorrow comes too slowly as I mill around this town
    I look to you and the government and feel you've let me down
I see myself humiliated as people of color struggling more than some
    Yesterday I was a human being and today you call me bum.

Don't call me a refugee because I am American and true blue
    Don't call me a refugee though slightly different from you
Don't call me a refugee though I am displaced for today
    Don't call me a refugee and look the other way.

I think about my brothers fighting in another land
    For freedom for our neighbors living on foreign sand
I think about the fathers over there fighting and many mothers, too
    I wonder how they feel about my treatment here with you.

They fight side by side with other Americans for freedom and democracy
    To protect our nation's borders, our air, land and sea
I am fighting for my life and watching others die
    Bodies floating down the river and all I can do is cry.

That could be me in minutes, hours, even days from right now
    I fall to my knees and close my eyes, hang my head and bow
I pray that the morning brings help with food and aid
    I ask forgiveness for my sins and all on the alter laid.

The hurricane hit and changed my life and my home was blown away
    The waters came and washed us out with no place else to stay
Yet, my faith is strong and I believe with God I can go on
    And someday will return to my family and happy home.

I live in a country that is proud and mighty in what we do
    Leadership is stalling, though, while depending on a few
Relief is stymied by confusion and lack of effective skills
    In coordinating the efforts and seeking money for the bills.

People shooting, raping, looting, and running here and there
    Busses coming and busses going with anarchy in the air
Choppers landing, people standing, others looking to the hills
    Some are fleeing, others seething with their broken wills.

I see people struggling to keep family members near
    I see people reaching out to help and being most sincere
I see people with open arms picking victims up
    I see people with helping hands passing around the cup

When I see survivors through the media and the picture reporters paint
    I wonder if they realize the many lives they taint
The words they use are powerful, sometimes demeaning and causing harm
    In reporting on events with candor and alarm.

Don't call me a refugee for I am an American and true blue
    Don't call me a refugee though slightly different from you
Don't call me a refugee though I am displaced for today
    Don't call me a refugee and look the other way.

Don't Fan the Flames of Racism

Don't fan the flames of racism
And start heating up the storm,
It may cost the lives of many
And bring nothing but great harm.

Don't stroke the minds of racists
And walk away and turn your back,
You may find yourself falling
Amidst a direct attack.

Don't leave yourself encumbered
With faulty rules and laws to bid,
Gather all around you and
Keep your children hid.

Don't think you've got the answers
And can see each other's heart,
When people speak of separation
And ways tearing us apart.

Don't assume you know your neighbors
Bordering on each and every side,
When the flood gates have sprung open
No longer moving with the tide.

Don't fan the flames of racism
And start heating up the storm,
It may cost the lives of many
And bring nothing but great harm.

Claudia Stuart
©1998

Enter into the Sanctuary The Shooter

Enter into the sanctuary
    Of peace and calm
Until it's not.

Trust in the Lord
    With thanksgiving
All you've got.

Look to the hills
    For salvation
To you and all.

Walk in the glory
    Of Jesus
Before the fall.

Hear the choirs
    Of angels
That's all around.

Enter the gates
    Of heaven
Upon that ground.

Everyday Is a New Day

Everyday is a new day
    With endless possibilities
    Opportunities of growth
    Room to stretch
    And boundaries to expand

Everyday presents a new chance
    For walking along the beach
    Making new friends
    Exploring new fields
    Approaching new destinations

Everyday harbors new challenges
    For expanding the mind
    Creating new venues
    Finding innovative solutions
    Walking new pathways

Everyday creates new delights
    Hearing different messages
    Seeking new arenas
    Watching distant labors and
    Harnessing the powers within

Everday creates new situations
    For communicating with others
    Sharing with others
    Believing in others
    Of what everyday

CStuart

God Love

Peering through the darkness. . .

Seeing the light of day. . .

On being me. . .

On being you. . .

Being in love. . .

With God above. . .

God's Love He Kept Me

As I prepare
    To meet my Master
When I have passed away

I think about the
    Many times
He kept me throughout the day.

When I was young
    And growing
He kept me on my path

To do the things
    The right way
Learning to read, write and math.

He helped me
    Tackle subjects
In classes long and short

He taught me how to
    Treat my friends
Even when to depart.

As I met
    My help mate
Within that faithful hour

He kept us strong to
    Withstand the odds
Completely within His power.

He made me quite
  The lady
What I was meant to be

As we went along
  Our way
Raising our family.

Together we were
  Stronger
Than living by ourselves

And we treasured
  All our time
And filling all our shelves.

The Lord has always
  Been so good to me
As I look upon those days

And changing obstacles
  In our path
Caused changes in our ways.

As we age together
  We have many
Different pleas

And draw closer to
  The Master
And stay upon our knees.

My days on earth
  Have ended
And I've reached those pearly gates

To join my Lord and Savior
  As I hope
For me He waits.

I'm honored to see
    My Master
As I trod upon these poor feet

I've prayed and lived
    For the moment
To be able to take my seat.

Thank you, Lord,
    You kept me
Through good times and the bad

You made my life
    Worth living
For this I am so glad.

My faith in You
    Never wavered
Nor floundered from my side

I never had to worry
    In life
And never had to hide.

Thank you, Lord,
    You kept me
Within your loving arms

From all hurt, harm
    And danger
Away from all alarms.

Now as my family
    Grows stronger
And tarries upon their way

Let them know You
    And remember
You keep all harm at bay.

For You are
    The Almighty
All knowing for everyone

Keep them also close
    To Thee
As their journey has just begun.

Thank you, Lord,
    You kept me
My life has been such fun

To live and be
    So happy
From evening 'til morning sun.

Gratitude

For every act of kindness
Shown to me and my
Penguins

I say thank you,
For I am grateful for your
Thoughts.

For every time you've shared
How much you really
Cared

I am grateful
And I thank you for your
Thoughts

For every time you have given
Me a book, to find the little penguins
On a page

I am thankful for you've fed me
And spurned me on
My way

To create a few more
Penguins in
A day.

For every time you've chatted
How penguins make you
Happy

You have fed me.

For every time you've shared
A new documentary, too
Of all the little black and whites around the world

You have fed me.

For every time you've called me
With a sighting that
You've had

You have fed me.

For every time you've mentioned
How delicate the birds
How utterly sweet they are and oh, those tiny feet!

You have fed me.

For every time you have brought me
Penguin socks for my feet, to stop the chill and
Brighten up my day.

You have fed me.

For all the little birds you
Have put onto
My path

You have fed me.

For building on my house
Was such an inspiration, too
For it allowed me to salvage along the way

Each and every piece of rock or stone
Or glass, or even
Shiny piece of clay

I have used it to its fullest
  From the shiniest to the dullest
    To create a work of art for my display

I am grateful for your kindness
  Every brick I've used to build
    And craft a collection of penguin artifacts.

To contractors and technicians,
  And housekeepers and clinicians
    I am grateful and I thank you from my heart.

The Lord has truly blessed me
  And I'm grateful everyday
    For all that He has done throughout my life.

So, to you, enjoy my penguins
  They are here but a short stay
    And I hope in some small measure

That they brighten up your day. Thank—you.

CStewart

Harness the Power

We need to gather
    And bundle it up,
Really harness the power.

Save it yet another day
    By the second
The minute and the hour.

Face each day as it comes
    Remembering what
To do.

It is important
    To stay on track,
Gaining benefits there for you.

Up the mountain of life
    You tread
To greet another day.

Harness the power you have within
    It will be much better
Without delay.

I See the World

I see the world
    Through your eyes
Faceless in a crowd

I hear the voices
    Of the tribe
Each and everyone allowed

I smell the
    Richness of your breath
Today and years to come

I taste the sweetness
    Of your voice
Though of a different drum

I walk in shoes
    Of which you walk
Down a crowded street

I see the eyes
    From which you speak
To everyone you meet

I touch the heart
    From deep within
Held close to make your way

I feel the thunder
    Of your feet
Going about your day

I hear the voices
    Of the past
Reverberating from side to side

I sense the mighty
    Roar inside
That makes you retreat and hide

I feel the music
    Of your soul
As you take a step

I hear the stories
    Yet untold
Your liveliness and pep

I see the joy
    Of being alive
Walking and talking and such

I sense the pride
    All over the place
For love of country, very much.

If Jesus Came Back into the World Today, Could I Afford to See Him? A Masterpiece

"All hail, all hail,
    Here comes the King."
I fight through the crowds
    To see what they mean.

A lady faints and
    Is trampled down
Because she wanted
    To see the crown.

Babies screaming
    With tired seats,
No one smiles
    And no one greets.

The youth hurl bottles
    Onto the streets,
Landing on many a
    Poor soul's feet.

Where is this Prince
    That I want to meet,
The Prince of Mercy,
    The Prince of Peace?

The huddled masses
    Push forward, some
Passing the side street
    Housing the bums.

Blood spurts forth
    From clawing hands,
Ministers walking with
    Black armbands.

The only light
    Comes from Heaven above,
Because in this flock
    You won't find love.

The center is meshed
    With security and police,
Monitoring each soul
    Entering from the street.

But what's this I faintly
    Hear in the wind?
Pay fifty dollars before
    You come in!

That's for each man,
    Woman and child.
They don't care if
    You've walked many a mile.

Pay up front and
    Don't delay,
Or you won't see
    Your Christ today.

Sick and forlorn,
    The crowd does scatter—
But, Christ springs forth asking,
    "What is the matter?

You dare charge my people
    This exorbitant fee?
For what, no one pays
    To come see me.

No mayor, no servant
    No peasant, no wife
Must pay me money
    To save their life.

Come, all my children,
    Rich and poor,
Just a pure heart will
    Open the door.

Love for your neighbor
    And foes between
Will banish all sin
    And leave you clean."

So, the doors opened wide
    And all could see,
No one must pay
    If you want to be free.

Silence fell upon the crowd
    As we listened to the call,
In a time long ago,
    Jesus paid it all.

I'm So Glad my God Loves Me

He loves me in my darkest hour
    And in the light of day

His love is all around me
    As I start upon my way

He greets me in the morning
    And folds me in at night

He soothes my every ache and pain
    Clears my vision and my sight

He makes me wonder as time passes on
    What is beneath the land and sky?

He gives me what I need in life
    No need to ask Him why

He feeds me with His holy word
    Leaves me wanting more

His grace is everlasting
    And evens out the score

He is my rock in ages past
    So sound and never changing

He lifts my spirit to higher heights
    Always rearranging

He meets me in the sunshine
Puts light upon my path

He removes the obstacles along the way
And truly calms my wrath

He loves me in the morning
Lasting throughout the day

He removes my enemies upon me
Blessing me along the way

He loves me as I'm longing
To create that which is right

He answers all my prayers in time
Keeps me in His sight

He is upon the hill
So wonderful and sublime

He is my coach in life
Always on my mind

He loves me in my darkest hour
And in the light of day

His love is all around me
As I start upon my way

He is even in my writing
Each stroke I make in time

He allows me to be creative
As I make my message rhyme

He guides my mind and memory
Of all He's done for me

He sparks my intuition
When I cannot see

He fuels my heart with love
    Sets my soul on fire

He moves me in a special way
    Inching me higher and higher

He causes me to look up
    For my health and strength

He puts food upon my plate
    And all that I can drink

He is a mighty God
    And God all by Himself

He is the Almighty Creator
    Manufacturer of the wealth

He made the highest mountains
    And the land and sea

He put the stars up in the sky
    He made you and me

He created the birds in the air
    And the fish within the sea

He made the mighty lions roar
    And the monkeys in the tree

He smoothed out valleys and hills galore
    Set volcanoes and islands, too

He had the crickets chirping
    Oh, what else did He do?

He put the earth on its course
    Set the time around

He loves everything from sea to sea
    And more that is not found

He loves me and I am so grateful
To be a child of His

He is my Holy Father
And knows that He is

He loves me in my darkest hour
And in the light of day

His love is all around me
As I start upon my way.

Diversity
C Stewart

It's a Mistake

It's a mistake to think you can't help somebody, reach out to the poor, acknowledge the existence of people different from yourself.

It's a mistake to be in a town that has a church on every corner, and other people don't look around, outside, down the street, next-door to understand people are poor and need help; food, shelter, love, kindness, generosity and the like.

It's a mistake to take what God has blessed you with and not see the need or the urgency to share with others less fortunate than ourselves.

It's a mistake to harbor bad feelings, ill will, towards those who are victims who see no way out.

It's a mistake not wanting to see the destruction, devastation, and death and not feel that we have a responsibility at all, not to let this happen again, and again, and again.

It's a mistake not to follow the common rules of decency and respect and honor for those individuals around you that look like you, and not like you, and so much like you, and so different from you.

It's a mistake not to have the concern and compassion for others to understand better their plight, their quest, their problems, their issues in life that you could probably help with if you cared.

It's a mistake not to honor families while struggling to put food on the table, clothes on their children, shelter from the storms, and living in utter devastation.

It's a mistake to look the other way, and say that you will obey, the Christian way to help save the day, yet do nothing.

It's a mistake not to understand what the families have at hand dealing with addictions of drugs, sex, food, lust, work, mindlessness, and not reach out and reach in.

It's a mistake not to care about the streets of our country as well as the streets of other countries and roads through the jungles and paths of ruin.

It's a mistake not to give of yourselves what has been given to you to use in the betterment of life as we know it.

It's a mistake not to take the hand of that young person and lead them, guide them, mentor them, help them, teach them to read, write, take care of themselves, and the world around them.

It's a mistake not to feed the poor, open the door, share the light, with all our might.

It's a mistake not to treat people the way you want to be treated and love your neighbor as you love yourself.

It's a mistake to think that we can survive in a world not caring for creatures large and small and the biggest of them all the land and water that surrounds us.

It's a mistake to think that we do not need to heed the clarion call that's made to all, to step up, step in, or step out.

It's a mistake not to acknowledge that we know what to do but won't do it. We know what to feel, and don't feel it. We know how to act, but don't do it. We know where to go but won't do it. We know we can do it but won't do it.

It's a mistake to attack and smear the very veneer of the statues upon the land we wish to preserve.

It's a mistake not to acknowledge that the time is now and the race is on, and if we are to finish at all, we must recognize we're in it to win it and united we stand, and divided we fall.

It's a mistake not to see the vision of generations to come and prevent some of the destructive ways, and dangerous pitfalls set before them.

It's a mistake not to turn this around, while we we're yet on the ground and can make judgments sound and purpose abound.

It's a mistake to wake up from dreaming and with all of the scheming have not found the meaning of changing the landscape and scenery in the world around us benefitting all.

It's Not Enough To Say, "I Love You"

It's not enough to
    Say, "I love you,"
And want me
    Night and day

It's not enough to
    Say, "I'm sorry,"
As you go on your
    Merry way.

I need more just
    To sustain me
With a kiss

I need more to
    Send my heart
Into a wedded bliss.

I need to hold you
    Wrap you tightly
With both my arms

I need to know
    You will protect me
From all danger, hurt and harm.

It's not enough to
    Say, "I love you,"
And want me
    Night and day

It's not enough to
    Say, "I'm sorry,"
As you go on your
    Merry way.

I need to know
    You'll be there for me
With all the passion
    In your loins

I need to know
    You really love me
My name across your heart
    Forever worn.

Jesus

I want to see my Jesus
He is a part of me

I want to be like Jesus
He is inside of me

I want to be with Jesus
He alone will guide me

I want to see my Jesus
He is a part of me.

Lazy Days of Summer

Lazy days of summer
  Swimming and boating
    And such

Running around and playing
  We like that
    Very much.

Ice cream, pies, and melon
  Fried chicken and
    Collard greens

Reunions and grand church
  Socials and others
    In between.

Dances and lots of parties
  Around on every
    Block

Who are all the members
  And who's not in
    The flock?

Children running to and fro
  Chased by larger
    Kids

Parents and grandparents
  And whomever else are
    Kin.

Hot, hot days and warm, warm nights
With moisture in
The air

No work, no school, no long
Range plans leaving us without
A care.

The days are long, the nights too short
For all we have
To do

To meet and greet each other
To say, "How do you
Do?"

Oh, the lazy days are over
Back to schedules and
Long plans

Say goodbye to all your
Neighbors and sounds
From the band.

The fun was great and splendid
It's over now it
Seems

Summer is brief—far too short
To carry on—if you know
What I mean.

Lies, Lies and More Lies

A lie falling trippingly from the tongue.
A lie at night when the day is done.

A lie spat out for days and days,
A lie that lingers in a haze.

A lie that swells and has no end.
A lie fresh off the button, send.

A lie that could maim or kill a few.
A lie so big and bold that others knew.

A lie from the most powerful source.
A lie that took the world off course.

A lie to set the record straight.
A lie prompting much debate.

A lie to withstand the test of time.
A lie not discerning the end of the line.

A lie that shocks and shatters lives.
A lie that cuts like a thousand knives.

A lie about the women and what they did.
A lie about disaster to keep the truth hid.

A lie about the numbers coming out of the gate.
A lie about people teaching generations to hate.

A lie about all manner of sex and such.
A lie about size, not so much.

A lie about the generals and the government as a whole.
A lie on the media as the cameras roll.

A lie about greatness and wanting to be thanked.
    A lie about how our society tanked.

A lie about the taxes and when they were paid.
    A lie about recovery as more bodies were laid.

A lie to the people and not great to run.
    A lie undeniably reckless later said as fun.

A lie about world health at a fever pitch.
    A lie about scientific plans disappearing in a ditch.

A lie on his imminence that time would not tell.
    A lie as the systems fade into hell.

A lie as the economy takes unlimited toll.
    A lie about war as stealth rumors unfold.

A lie that floats throughout endless seas.
    A lie that flies and stings like bees.

A lie of such vicious, vile and evil stuff.
    Lies, lies, lies—enough, enough!

Lord I See You

Lord, I see you
I hear you
I taste you.
Lord, I see you
I smell you
I feel you.
Lord, I see you
I sense you
I touch you.

As I look across this vast land,
I see most of your kingdom.

As I listen to the ocean waves smashing in the sea,
I hear your voice of reason this, my child, take care of me.

As I watch the cattle in the distance dotted here and there,
I hear you whisper softly, do not harm, nary a hair.

As I gaze outside my window each day and night,
I see people walking and children playing, never to leave my sight.

As I watch the railroad crossing and the trains going to and fro,
I see you in the midst as I watch the flow.

As I think of all the creatures that you have placed in front of me,
I see your hands work on the future meant to be.

As I see people scurrying over here and there,
I see you ordering, instructing and guiding people everywhere.

As I see places of worship standing tall against the sky,
I see them also crumbling, falling, closing, and I ask, why?

As I listen to the chatter, the clatter, and the clangs,
I hear you in the midst of it, and hear others sing.

As my ears detect a voice so loud it makes me stop,
I hear your echo in the wind and hasten to let it drop.

As I hear the world a spinning off its axis and maybe more,
I wonder if it is you again saying, that is for sure.

As I hear you in the breeze placing leaves up on my face,
I remember why you kept reminding me of your grace.

I hear you Lord, my master, telling me tried and true,
To love, honor and obey you, that is what I must do.

I hear anguish all around me, some are fit and some not so,
I hear of death and destruction of the ones we must let go.

I hear you all around me and through the silence know,
To bend my knees and thank you because you told me so.

As I witness people dying, crying, trying to make things right,
I taste you in my tears and never far from my sight.

As I drink the water to replenish and eat food for nourishment,
I thank you for the raindrops and the rivers that you sent.

As I savor all the blessings each and every day,
I thank you evermore and bow my head to pray.

As we share bread and bounty so ripe up on the land,
We are thankful for it all as it goes from hand to hand.

Lord, I taste the sweetness and the goodness of all you have made for me.
The fruits of your labor are all it is meant to be.

Lord, I smell you in the orchards, vineyards, and green gardens filled with dew,
And as I get that whiff of air, I say, Lord, it is really you.

I smell you in the lake beds, in the meadows so divine.
I smell you in the ocean with coral reefs and lime.

I smell you throughout the gateways, traveling from place to place,
Being constantly reminded, this is God 's grace.

I smell you as the people gather in destinations near and far,
Places reached by land and sea and others reached by car.

I smell you in the voices as people moan and groan and cry,
Begging again the question, why did you let them die?

I feel you in the raging floods, tsunamis and much, much more.
I feel the water thrashing hard against the shore.

I feel your mighty power, Lord, as buildings crash up on the ground.
Creatures scurrying and battling about, and bodies never found.

I feel you in the heartbeat of each passerby.
I feel you in the sunshine drifting from the sky.

I feel you in the urgency sweeping across the earth,
Constantly reminding all to put God first!

I feel you in hostility, warring factions here and there,
Those dividing and controlling, banishing without care.

I feel you in tranquility, a calming sight to see.
You reaching out and saying, let go and let me lead.

I feel you driving forces to meet each and every need,
Diminishing hopeless frustration, doing away with greed.

I feel the comfort in knowing of each and every touch,
That you are saying how much you love us, oh, so very much.

I sense you all around us to be kind and grateful, too,
For all that you have given and promises anew.

I sense you in the pulpit with your guidance and favor about,
With messages of unity, faith, hope, and charity, throughout.

I sense you upon waking from sleeping the night away,
Meeting me in the morning, keeping all fears at bay.

I sense you in the big book, the Bible as I read,
The power of forgiveness, love, and the mustard seed.

I sense you as I greet strangers upon my path.
I sense you in thoughts, words, deeds, and the aftermath.

I sense you in the forest filled with many trees.
I sense you in the wind and the ocean breeze.

I sense you in the gutters among all kinds of folk.
I sense you in the subways among people reading notes.

I sense you in the voices of people large and small.
I sense you in the crowds in the meeting halls.

I sense you in the schoolyard as children play, climb, and run.
I sense you in the ceremony with the beating drum.

I sense you in the jungle as creatures surviving, harking to the distant call.
I sense you in the cities and suburbs, people shuffling through the malls.

As I gaze upon the raindrops and feel the snow upon my face,
I feel your gentle touch and bask in your grace.

As I swim in the water and feel sand upon my feet.
I feel your touch around me, I feel the sun and heat.

As I shake hands with my neighbor and greet them with a smile,
I feel your touch within me that stays with me a while.

As I see all in your image with love and kindness, too,
I feel your touch upon us telling us what we must do.

Your touch will guide us in the right ways to go,
Our steps will lead to many we may not know.

Your touch will direct us to be all that we can be,
Showing love and compassion to all that we see.

Your touch is so mighty, your majesty so complete,
You will never leave us, your love, so tender and sweet.

Lord is Worthy

He is just too wonderful
    Not to do what He asks of us

He is just too powerful
    Not to render Him our trust

He is just too merciful
    Not to be thankful for kindness, too

He is just too bountiful
    Not to make us anew

He is just too sustaining
    Not to fulfill our needs

He is just too beautiful
    Not to be worthy of our deeds

For the Lord is worthy
    So very, very worthy

And He alone deserves
    Our all in all.

Love

Love is filling that
Deep pit in your heart and
Having it teaming over with
Hot, sticky, gooey, and gushy
Firmament.

Love is wanting to be held and
Swelled and devoured and scoured and
Scalded and overwhelmed by that
Other person.

Love is wonderful, beautiful, luscious and
Lively and joyous
Jovial and
Fantastic.

Love is being one
In that moment in time
Through the period to
Get to the place
Called home.

West Texas A&M University
Go Buffs

Love, Perhaps

Don't tell me that you love me and
    Don't listen to my pain.
Don't tell me that you love me and
    Leave me standing in the rain.

Don't tell me that you love me and
    Look the other way
Searching to find another place,
    Another person and even another day.

Don't tell me that you love me
    And look into my past.
Don't tell me that you love me and
    That our love will not last.

Don't tell me that you love me and
    Don't listen to my pain.
Don't tell me that you love me and
    Leave me standing in the rain.

Mean Streets

Don't tell me about mean streets.

Don't tell me about mean streets where you find death and destruction, construction, illusions, delusions and devastation.

Don't tell me about mean streets where people live everyday walking, talking, stalking and barking at each other along the way toward liberation.

Don't tell me about mean streets where people hide, inside, outside, right side, left side, and under the awnings of the stores and hotels, motels, Holiday Inns, and the like.

Don't tell me about mean streets where the man was pulled from his ride, knocked down on his side by policeman taking his life.

Don't tell me about mean streets because I'll have to tell you what happened next that the man died before our eyes, in broad daylight.

Don't tell me about mean streets where people gathered in huge numbers to pay homage to the man that died on his side with that officer's knee on his neck.

Don't tell me about mean streets and the billowing, ferocious fire leaping to the middle of Main Street and the side street, and the long street, and the short street and the police department.

Don't tell me about mean streets when the National Guard marched to disperse the crowd that had gathered for the man that was on his side with the officer's knee on his neck and he died.

Don't tell me about mean streets where there is no justice and no peace. Let the jury deliberate and see where the fate of the four officers lies.

Don't tell me about mean streets where people for whatever consequences they may bear have their day in the streets and their voices heard.

Don't tell me about mean streets unless you have a solution to the revolution up and down the avenues all around cities and suburbs.

Don't tell me about mean streets where the lives of George Floyd, Trayvon Martin, Ahmaud Arbery, Breonna Taylor, Sandra Bland, and Amadou Diallo. Yes, call their names, Eric Garner, Tamir Rice, James Byrd, Jr., Emmett Till, Jimmie Lee Jackson, and many more were lost.

Don't tell me about mean streets because I already know it's going to take Divine Intervention to make the corrections and set things right, at great cost.

Don't tell me about mean streets.

Moments

Savor the moments of
Quiet bliss
And allow the mind
To explore.

Vistas of opportunity
Are abound
And truly so
Much more.

Wallow in the excitement
Of the range
Of movement in
The universe.

Quietly fathom
The endless possibilities
Awaiting the intensive
Exploration of ideas.

Soaking in rays of
Rhythmic motion
With the ebb
And flow of plenty.

So much to do
And a dream
Come true.

Savor the moments of
Quiet bliss
And allow the mind
To explore.

Moments II

There in the window
I see you.
How I long to hear you.
Feel you
Touch you
Heal you.

There in the window
We are gone.

My Boys Are Gone

My boys are gone
    To another city
And I miss them so.
    Shall I tell them?

They have moved on
    To a life away
In a far off place.
    Shall I call them?

The dreams are there
    To have and hold
To be fulfilled, still.
    Shall I remind them?

How they have grown up
    Such nice young men
So strong and oh, so tough.
    Shall I show them?

They have such courage
    And free to be
Whomever they choose to be.
    Shall I call them?

Time goes on
    God is in control
The remote is there on the dash.
    Shall I remind them?

My boys are gone
    To another place
Up the road a piece.
    Shall I find them?

I miss them so
    Just so they know
In time, we will be together, again.
    Shall I tell them?

I love them now
    As in the past
And more and more each day
    Shall I call them?

The joy we share
    Knowing they are there
Down the street.
    Shall I remind them?

The stories we told
    The tales of old
Imagination running away.
    Shall I tell them?

Concentration, too
    Other games anew
Competition the order of the day.
    Shall I show them?

All in a days rest
    They are the best
Just ask and they will reply.
    Shall I call them?

My boys are gone
    To another city
And I miss them so.
    Shall I tell them?

CStuart

My Mother May on My Mother's Day

My mother may on my Mother's Day
Write me, text me, call me
Tell me you're okay.

And if you can't do all that
Whisper that you love me
And that will make my day.

When I close my eyes, I see you in a certain kind of way
There beside me, with me
All along the way.

My mother may on my Mother's Day.
My day is brighter, my heart is wider
God is still on the throne.

I will be fine, even at this time
You're safe, secure
At peace, at home.

Write me, text me, call me to make me feel complete.
The Lord says to you it's time to rest
Come here and take your seat.

My mother may on my Mother's Day.

My Reality

I make it up as
    I go along
Just like everyone
    Else.

Somewhere in there
    I'll hear a song
I made it up
    Myself.

I leap for joy
    As I think aloud
Praise God for everything.

I make it up as
    I go along
Just like everyone
    Else.

New Citizens' Address
I Come Here

I come here to share
I come here to shine
I come here to sing
I come here to dine

I come here to sing
I come here to play
I come here to say
I come here to pray

Now is the time
    For all you men
To come to the
    Aid of your country

I say

Now is the time
    For all you ladies
To come to the
    Aid of your country

I come from Egypt
I come from Milan
I come from Russia
I come from Ceylon

I come from the east
I come from the west
I come from the north
I come from the south

As the wind blows
    I come
As the storm snows
    I come

As the bells ring
    I come
As the birds sing
    I come

As the sea billows
    I come
Through wind in the willows
    I come

Sun high in the sky
    I come
Meet you by and by
    I come

Glad to be here
Have some cheer here
Grab a chair here
Stay a year here

Guten Tag
    Buenos Diaz
G—day mate, Konnichi wa
    How ya doin'

Hello
    Hi
Boy, howdy
    Ta Ta

Hear ye, Hear ye
My name is Claudia Stuart
And I am glad to see you

Thank you, thank you
For having me here, today.
Welcome to America!

To the land of good and plenty!

To the most amazing country in the world!

You have the opportunity to be a part of this vast, wonderful and diverse country. We enjoy a lot of amenities here like different kinds of food; different kinds of scenery—whether you are on the east coast or the west; the north or the south; or just plan to live in this great State of Texas. There is a lot to see here.

We have people coming here from all over the world that have settled here and raised a generation of family and enjoyed their friends, also. You might have come because you have family or friends here that wanted you to come and live. All together to reap the benefits of living in a free society. You have a lot of freedoms—here. Freedom to move about; work for an employer of your choosing; worship in whatever religion you honor; buy whatever you can afford; partake of the arts and entertainment when available. You might want to star in something yourself.

I have traveled around to many lands and met a lot of interesting people and visited exciting places. Whether it was Europe or South America; parts of the Caribbean or Hawaii; or close like Mexico or Canada, all have their own style and culture and uniqueness. I guess what I can appreciate about living here in America, is that we have many, many interesting people of many different cultures and ethnic groups and we have a lot of places of interest—all rolled into one.

We have a government interested in the lives of its people. We have law enforcement to keep our communities safe and secure. You do not want to be caught on the wrong side of the law. We have a vast infrastructure of clean running water, flushing toilets, heating and air conditioning, paved streets and roadways, bridges over land and water, new buildings, old buildings, churches, cathedrals, synagogues, schools, colleges and universities, and parks and massive sports arenas, and city transportation to points all over this town. We have buses, planes and trains to also take you where you want to go. We have jobs, jobs, jobs! We have a lot and we find that we do not mind paying our own way for the kind of lifestyle we enjoy.

Come and live among us. Come and be a productive member of our society. As a citizen, you now have that opportunity. Take advantage of that for only you can make your stay in America something that you can be proud of now and for generations to come.

I am so proud to be an American living, working and making my life here what I want it to be.

Share poem here:
"Let Me Be"

Let me be
Free to be
Whatever I
Want to be

Let me live
All my life
What I want
It to be

Let me guide
My own course
And make
My own mistakes

Let me have
The sole chance
To be me
For goodness sakes

Let me fly
Throughout the world
Seeing what I
Want to see

Let me be
Free to be
Whatever I
Want to be.

©1984
By Claudia Stuart

Dream big and you will find that to fulfill your dreams, you must start with a single step. You are taking that step today. The walk of life will be only what you make it. I wish you luck and good fortune and again, welcome to America.

CStuart

No Time for Mess

Don't talk to me now
    For I've no time
To be bothered with
    Your mess.

Give me a break
    And you move on
Using others to
    Fill your nest.

Try as you may
    I'll not succumb
To play the games
    With you.

Seek revenge
    Without a twinge
Will all come back
    On you.

I seek a higher
    Calling
Sticking to my
    Plan.

You are confused
    And therefore
Cannot possibly
    Understand.

The need to rise
    And soar above
Little minds
    And big, big faults.

Trusting in the One
    Above
Relieving all cares
    And wants.

I've no time
    To dilly dally
Like I've got
    All day

I must move on
    Without malady
Getting in
    My way.

Time is of
    The essence
The beat goes on
    They say.

Keep your eye
    On the prize
Let nothing get
    In the way.

Wasting time
    Is not a choice
That I will make
    Today.

Clear my head
    Move away
Time is up
    And out of play.

CStuart

Ode to Amarillo

It started out as just, Ragtown,
Because of all the dust and dirt
Upon the ground
And all around.

Stir up the wind,
Listen to the sound
And the mighty roar.
See all unbound.

No grass nor trees to sustain it.
No buildings nor mountains
To contain it.
Nothing there to frame it.

So, let the wind blow
Etching out crevices in the land.
The bright yellow way
Like the yellow hued sand.

The land glistening in the rays of
The sun in the big sky.
Home of creatures large and small
From buffalo to the prairie dog until they die.

Looking out as far as you can see,
The vast land meeting the horizon.
Buffalo roaming, slowly moving away.
Native culture now, long gone.

Amarillo it came to be
Made of dirt and grit.
Pioneers edged here, too.
Inking out land and claiming it.

As we go throughout the day
With everything we've learned,
We know that specifically along the way,
Are the successes that we've earned.

If you live in Amarillo,
Come what may
Day by day
You've got to stay.

Passion

Waiting for the pleasure
    Of seeing your smile, again
Hoping no more loneliness
    Defeating hours of strain

The joy of us together
    Transcending our delight
Coping with the future
    Through each day and night

Living for the moment
    To shed a fantasy
Over the sea of anguish
    To complete ecstasy

Your face appears in memories
    The touch marking the spot
What a dream filled victory
    Such moments, sizzling hot.

Power Down

Death and destruction all around

And we are dealing with a clown.

Power Up

I want to reach out and let you know that I see you. I hear your voice in the wind. I want to touch you and see your sweet smile and acknowledge that you are there. I see you all around me and your presence is overwhelming.

I see you in the streets and know that is not the best place for you, yet you are there. The cars are no longer speeding by your way and the people have gone home.

I see that you are first on the scene, again. Torrential rains could not keep you away. I want to tell you that your importance is tremendous, and you have your day.

I see you in the comfort of your home not being able to come out, just yet. I hear the sirens in the distance and know that we are not there, just yet. The time waits for no one and the foe acts swiftly.

I see that it touches everyone, and no one, and someone, and anyone, and that one, and this one. It makes its way harshly through the night, devastating families in its wake. We must contain it. Kill it. Destroy it. Banish it from the earth.

I see you desperately trying to put food on the table. Gathering your young around to feed them, coax them, teach them, protect them, save them. I see the frantic attempts by everyone to heed the clarion call to action.

I see death, destruction, despair, and devastation linger in the air over here and over there, yes, everywhere. The area is full of chills and spills and kills. Heavy is the load. Heavy is the burden. Heavy is the cost. Yes, heavy is the price we must pay.

I see the reckoning all around us. Yes, the corrections are being made. I see the vast and wide opening above us and that mighty hand reaching down. I see the world looking up, paying attention.

I see tons of people mesmerizing, recognizing, mobilizing, spiritualizing. The mighty hand of God is in control. The world is in a tailspin, yet, the mighty presence of our Lord is about the business of the day, the order of the day.

His will be done. His will be done.

Press Down Harder, An American Tragedy

Press down harder on his neck.
The policeman did without regret.
Remove the knee, was the distant call
The officer let the Black man fall.

I can't breathe.
I can't breathe.
They're killing me, Momma.
Momma, help me, Momma.

What happened next
Was tragic to see.
George Floyd died
There in the street.

We witnessed what happened.
We heard his cry.
Oh! Why did we let
This Black man die.

In broad daylight,
On a sunshiny day,
There, we let
His body lay.

It was hard to watch
Even that day,
And now it seems,
It won't go away.

Day in and day out,
From sunup to sundown,
We see yet, another
Black brother down.

Rain Dance

Raindrops dripping from my hair being tossed about in the midnight air.

I contemplate my next move as I turn the volume up as the music modulates in my ears.

I leap towards the sky as the water streams down my back and flicks off my elbows as my arms slowly descend by my sides.

My knees hit the ground in a swishing sound as the stars twinkle across the darkened sky.

Up again on my toes making tiny circles as the wet blades of grass lay crushed beneath my feet.

The rain drops bouncing off my thighs in the rhythm of the night as the full moon shines radiant light upon my path.

I slip and I slide.

I swing, sway and glide from

Side to side.

The music crescendos to the end as I twirl, yet again.

Just dancing naked in the rain.

Respect and Serve

How do you respect someone
    When they are shooting you to the ground?
        You don't.

How do you respect someone
    As they hurt and maim you when others aren't around?
        You don't.

How do you respect someone
    While they treat you with such disdain?
        You don't.

How do you respect someone
    Who doesn't bother to know your name?
        You don't.

How do you respect someone
    Who hunts you down in cold blood?
        You don't.

How do you respect someone
    Who does not earn your trust?
        You don't

You could see me as a person
    Say "Hello" and build a friend.
        You won't.

You could treat me as a brother
    And our struggling streets to defend.
        You won't.

You could help and aid others
    Whose lives are in distress.
        You won't.

You could protect and serve in ways
    That bring respect and honor and not neglect.
        You won't.

You could find a pathway to understanding
    Seeing my children in yours.
        You won't.

You could be a better person
    Shielding all communities at your doors.
        You won't.

Put Christ first in our hearts
    And in our minds.
        We will.

See in others what we honor, respect
    And can rebuild.
        We will.

Carry trust and love around
    As a mantle for respect.
        We will.

Foster caring and understanding and
    Build bridges without regret.
        We will.

Open doors of opportunity for all to live,
    Learn and work together.
        We will.

Respect and serve each other. . .
    Black lives matter; your lives matter; all lives matter.
        We will.

Sing a Song

Sing me a song,
    Diana Ross,
Make more
    History.

I can relate
    To all your
        Songs,
Baby Love
    And more,
        You'll see.

Sam Cooke
    Was so
Delightful,
    With Cupid and
Many more.

Sitting on the
    Dock of the
        Bay
With Otis Redding,
    What a
        Score.

Thriller with
    Michael Jackson,
Swinging to the
    Beat.

My Girl, by the
    Temptations and
        Mary Wells,
Without
    Defeat.

Going to the Chapel,
By the Shirelles,
About love and things,
Diana, you're in the
Movie about
How the Lady Sings.

Oh, sing me
A song
Diana Ross.
Sing it
Loud
Clear.

Isaac Hayes
Will come out
Of chains,
Then we
All will
Cheer.

Billie Holliday
Was a great
One, too,
Marvin Gaye
Was the
Best.

There are many songs of
Those great ones
Who have been
Laid to rest.

Tina Turner
Is on fire and
Dancing in the Street,

The Vandella's
Make you holler
Mashed potatoes
With your feet.

Stevie Wonder
Is a pro,
Quincy Jones
Is, too.

Music, dance
And singing,
So action-packed
For you.

What is the music
Ringing loudly
In my ear?

Turn the volume up
Real loud,
I want all the
World to hear.

Midnight Train to
Georgia
By Gladys Knight
And those great Pips.

Smokey Robinson
And the Miracles,
With songs to
Make you dip.

Patti LaBelle is
Wailing,
What a great act.

And Satchmo
With his trumpet
Out there,
Leading the pack.

Oh, the many records
On the floor
In front of me.

The memories that
    I cherish
And the song,
    Let It Be.

Sing those songs
    Diana Ross,
Sing them loud
    And clear,
All are gifted
    Melodies
And I collect them here.

Smile

Smile and the world
    Smiles with you
Frown and you cry alone

Joy and the pathways
    Open
To build a happy home.

Smile for your hearts
    Contentment
Frown with your head hung low

Happy for the joy
    Within you
Making friends wherever you go.

Circle of Friends

So, You Love Me

So, you hold me on a pedestal
    And cater to my every
        Need

But, you cannot say I love you
    And do not see
        The Need.

So, you call me beautiful
    And are delighted by
        My smile

Yet, cannot say I love you
    Though, truly you are
        Beguiled.

So, you tinker with my fantasies
    And my every
        Wish indeed

And cannot say I love you
    Though it is love
        In need.

So, you are filled with laughter
    And giddiness
        Inside

But, cannot say I love you
    Those words you seem to
        Hide.

So, you move on my command
    And come running to
        My side

Yet, cannot say I love you
As your nose is
Opened wide.

So, you speak of future dreams
And look to the sky
So blue

But, cannot say I love you
And to your heart
Be true.

So you spend hour after hour
In restless
Despair

Yet, cannot say I love you
Or even that
You care.

So, you long to be with me
Though many miles
Away

Yet, cannot say I love you
And be with me
Today.

So, you hold me on a pedestal
And cater to my every
Need

But, you cannot say I love you
And do not see
The need.

Well, I love you

CStuart

March of the Penguins

Stop the Violence, Stop it

They were Asian women
Walking to their fate.
Who knew they would be taken down
Because of their race.

It is happening all around us.
I see it in her smile.
She will not last a day,
Nor walk another mile.

Stop the violence, stop it
Stop the killings, drop it.
See it happening, stop it
Say the words, drop it.

It hurts to the core
And so much more
To settle the score
In ways to ignore.

Hate is not the answer.
Killing is not desired.
Written down in history,
Leaving us uninspired.

Black, brown, red, yellow, and white,
All beautiful in God's sight.
Preserve the image with your might.
Lead with love, not fight or flight.

Not racism, sexism, nor ageism, too,
Anti-Semitism, a one to include,
Not bigotry nor prejudice.
Stop the violence, stop it.

Stop the violence, stop it
Stop the killings, drop it.
See it happening, stop it.
Say the words, drop it.

System's Failure

A tear in the system
A break in the dam

This will cause friction
Leading up to a scam

Plug up the holes
Set the levy straight

Use all the forces
And close the gate

The storm will be coming
Make no mistake

Rain clouds are bursting
Sealing the fate

Shut down the cables
Send out the alert

Fire power is mounting
Cover with dirt

The hills will be covered
With dust and debris

Shifts with no changes
No one is free.

CStewart

Thankful for the Harvest

We come today to say thank you
For all that God has done.
The race to bring the Harvest in
Has been a long and tedious run.

Thankful for the Harvest
To be shared from coast to coast
In the fields of good and plenty
Who cares who has the most?

The Lord has graciously provided
For you and all your kin
Not to give and share around the way
Would truly be a sin.

Now, we can feed the children
Our work is not in vain
Thank God for the land in which we live
And thank Him for the rain.

I grow potatoes
You grow corn
Peas, greens and apples
From the seeds
We have thrown.

As we worked the fields this year
The struggles came and went
We didn't know about the wheat and grain
Nor how our days were spent.

Yet, we are thankful for the Harvest
We now reap what we have sown.
Look at this beautiful, bountiful Harvest
With His Helping Hands we've grown.

The Perfect Gift

It took a while to
Think about what would
Truly make you happy.

That gold pocket watch
Was the perfect gift.

It keeps accurate time.

It is hard to get in
To set the time, you know.

It is encased in gold
And is simply stunning.

But, the watch was
Merely a symbol
In my eyes.

More was about the planning
And forethought I put in
Finding the perfect piece.

It was the love and attention
I gave to detail in planning even
The occasion for which
To deliver this gift.

It was the desire on my
Part to give you something special
And wonderful and
Something timeless.

It was the interest in
Getting it to you
In a timely manner.

It was that now at long last
I remembered
Your birthday.

Now comes the moment of
The much anticipated deliverance
On my part.

To hand it over and share
With you the story of
This great find.

And to see the spark of
Interest as you listened keenly
Hanging onto my every word.

The build up I gave
Kept you waiting with
Baited breath for this
Time piece.

You took it,
Gazed upon it.
Held it with such care and
Tenderness.

And looked into my moistened eyes
To say . . .
Thank you, Baby.
I love you.

The White Hat

The white hat
    For those who
Ride out into the sunset
    Doing a lot of good
For others

The white hat
    Bringing peace and justice
For the downtrodden, defenseless,
    Disenfranchised and disadvantaged
Among us

Yes, we know about the
    White hat
Few have worn it in the fullness of itself
    To serve others
In the spirit of love and brotherhood

This is a white hat
    Of a different kind

Still for the one who serves
Still for the one who cares

Still for the one who dedicates his life to Christ
Still for the one committed to God's Holy Word

Still for the man who stands tall
Still for the man with convictions

The white hat.

Time Flies

Don't go.
Did I tell you
How much I love you.

Did I tell you about
The good ole days.

You remember.

Too Long in the Shadows

Too long in the shadows
    Now, come into the light
You fought long and
    Hard to get here
Such power and such might.

You seem like such
    A natural
Proven service in good stead
    Taking control and a foothold
Being no longer lead.

You are here and
    You deserve it
Your life seems quite complete
    Your wife, your girl, your little tot,
My, what a mighty feat.

Travel

How I love to travel
Visiting places
Here and there,

Meeting a lot
Of People
Entering without a care.

To see those
Lives suspended
In jollity and fun,

To share the hearts
Of many
Under the evening sun.

To go into the
Rain forests
In Americas, north and south,

To see those
With plenty
And even more without.

Causes one to
Ponder
As we go along our way,

To remember to
Give back
You've seen a brighter day.

As we move along
The coastline
The terrain expanding quite a bit,

To see the climate
    Changes
        And what we do to fit.

Around the globe
    By morning
        Another world by mid-day,

Keeps you ever
    So humble
        And on your knees to pray.

How I love
    To travel
        Bright and early on my way,

Another person,
    Another valley
        Another surf, another bay.

Learning yet
    Another language
        To communicate our plan,

To see the beach
    And eat some fish,
        Slippery feet in the sand.

Embracing different
    Cultures
        More music and much dance,

Puts one in a
    Better mood
        To give others a chance.

Oh, I do love
    To travel
        Lying in the bright sunshine,

Makes me really
    Thankful
        That my life is so sublime.

Treasures

I search the world
    For treasures
Some big and some
    So small
In quaint, little
    Boutiques
Some in gigantic malls.

But all the treasures
    That I find
That truly catch my eye
    Still don't compare
To the one I have
    With you there
By my side.

Joy

Turn Away from Sorrow

Turn away from sorrow
  Turn away from pain
Don't dwell on tomorrow
  Enjoy first the rain.

Time will truly tell
  What is wise for you to know
Take the pieces of today
  Wherever you wish to go.

The path is being laid
  As you take a step
Walk the straight and narrow
  For promises to be kept.

Fulfill each day with joy
  That you feel inside
The world is there to draw on
  That you cannot hide.

Count your blessings daily
  Thankful for the best
Relying on past experiences
  Believing you've passed the test.

Turn away from sorrow
  Turn away from pain
Don't dwell on tomorrow
  Enjoy first the rain

CStuart

Unique

"Try to fit in,"
The round peg said
When approached
By the square box

"Your corners are
Tight and rigid,
You'll need to
Trim a lot.

A Tuck here,
A split there,
Round the shoulders
Make a grin. . ."

"Why not accept me
As I am?"
The box said
From within.

"If you see me as
You are—
With my
Differences, too,

You'll be pleasantly
Surprised to know
How much I am
Like you.

My sides may
Not be rounded
And I can't roll
On my way.

Yet, I like you the
    Way you are
And accept you
    Without delay.

Though our gait
    May be unbalanced
As we go rickety
    Down the street,

Our voice can still
    Be as one
Even though
    Both unique."

Van Gogh

Starry, starry nights
Wind songs and café
Fields of wheat and yellow
Three ships in the bay.
Trees along the pathways
People in the pub
Painting in the yard
And, who is in the mug?

©1998

What Do You Want from Me

You want to be loved
So boldly and so free

You want to be held
Especially by me

You want to caress me
Show me that you care

You want me in the wind
Knowing that I am there

You want to be near me
Smiling in my eyes

You want honesty
Freedom from all lies

You want to control me
Taking me for yourself

You want me on a pedestal
Kept high upon the shelf

You want to love me
Deep into the night

You want to love me
Until the dawning light

You want to laugh with me
Humor that will sell

You want me to send goodies
To you through the mail

You want to be near me
By my side at night

You want to hold me
Squeeze me with your might

You want my body
Use it for yourself

You want the passion
Restoring thus the wealth

You want me
So special and carefree

You want me
Just yours to be

You want me
You want me.

Where Is the Outcry

Where is the outcry
    The sense of moral decency?

Where is my child?
    I will keep her safe
    I will protect her
    I will let no harm
        Come upon her.

Where is my brother?
    We are still his keeper
    We are still his protector
    We are still to let no harm
        Come upon him.

Where are my people?
    We are not stones in the sand
    We hear
    We see
        We act.

Where is our dignity?
    We must do what is right
    We must act when others do not
    We must act because
        We are human and decent
        And moral.

Where is the outcry
    When another is being destroyed
    Punched and kicked about
    In a knotted twist and flat?

Where is the outcry
When we sit back
And watch
And do nothing?

Where is the outcry
Because my soul
Is hurting for
My fellow man?

Where is the shame
I see in your eyes
As you look
Back at me?

Claudia Stuart
©1998

Wrap Me

Wrap me in your arms
    In your arms
    In your arms

Whisper in my ears
    Tender words
    Tonight.

Keep me by your side
    Holding me
    Real tight.

Wrap me in your arms
    In your arms
    In your arms.

Tell me you love me
    Oh, just me and you
Share with me your life
    Together so true.

Wrap me in your arms
    In your arms
    In your arms.

CStuart

Part II
Prose

Today Is a Great Day and Too Good to Be Quiet for 365 Days and More

Today is a great day to start celebrating each other.

Today is another great day to love one another.

Today is a great day to be kind to one another.

Today is a great day to help one another.

Today is a great day to show compassion for each other.

Today is a great day to respect one another.

Today is a great day to heal one another.

Today is a great day to have empathy for each other.

Today is a great day to be more understanding of each other.

Today is a great day to listen to each other.

Today is a great day to communicate with each other.

Today is a great day to pray for one another.

Today is a great day to treat others with dignity and respect.

Today is a great day to honor each other.

Today is a great day to cherish one another.

Today is a great day to aid one another.

Today is a great day to be there for one another.

Today is a great day to be more considerate of others.

Today is a great day to hold each other in high esteem.

Today is a great day to foster a good attitude toward others.

Today is a great day to hold others in high regard.

Today is a great day to recognize the humanity in others.

Today is a great day to find comfort in the presence of others.

Today is a great day to embrace the lives of others.

Today is a great day to embrace the differences of others.

Today is a great day to connect with others.

Today is a great day to socialize with others.

Today is a great day to greet one another.

Today is a great day to meet one another.

Today is a great day to lift others up as we climb.

Today is a great day to find one another.

Today is a great day to become acquainted with one another.

Today is a great day to believe in one another.

Today is a great day to make peace with each other.

Today is a great day to honor the dignity in each other.

Today is a great day to treasure each other.

Today is a great day to recognize others.

Today is a great day to care about each other.

Today is a great day to spread a little good will toward others.

Today is a great day to share laughter together.

Today is a great day to be courteous to others.

Today is a great day to start again with others.

Today is a great day to spread a little cheer with others.

Today is a great day to be more positive with others.

Today is a great day to seek allies of others.

Today is a great day to appreciate the goodness in others.

Today is a great day to recognize the diversity in others.

Today is a great day to make friends with others.

Today is a great day to make friends with someone different from yourself.

Today is a great day to mentor others.

Today is a great day to share with others.

Today is a great day to acknowledge others.

Today is a great day to reconnect with others.

Today is a great day to reconcile with others.

Today is a great day to uplift others.

Today is a great day to applaud others.

Today is a great day to accommodate others.

Today is a great day to receive others.

Today is a great day to work with others.

Today is another great day to spend time with others.

Today is a great day to seek common ground with each other.

Today is a great day to find happiness with each other.

Today is a great day to like each other.

Today is a great day to accept one another.

Today is a great day to welcome each other.

Today is a great day to trust one another.

Today is a great day to keep one another close.

Today is a great day to admire one another.

Today is a great day to praise one another.

Today is a great day to support one another.

Today is another great day to be more tolerant of others.

Today is a great day to serve others.

Today is a great day to advocate for others.

Today is a great day to stand for others.

Today is a great day to join others.

Today is a great day to unite with others.

Today is a great day to include others.

Today is a great day to treat others as you want to be treated.

Today is a great day to walk in the shoes of another.

Today is a great day to see yourself in others.

Today is a great day to see others in yourself.

Today is a great day to be good to others.

Today is a great day to reach out to others.

Today is a great day to assist others.

Today is another great day to have each other's back.

Today is a great day to encourage others.

Today is a great day to enhance the lives of others.

Today is a great day to be there for others.

Today is a great day to be present in the lives of others.

Today is a great day to have a stake in the lives of others.

Today is a great day to help rehabilitate the lives of others.

Today is a great day to help restore good conditions in the lives of others.

Today is a great day to teach someone to read and write.

Today is a great day to teach someone a new skill.

Today is a great day to reinforce good practices in the lives of others.

Today is a great day to help improve the lives of others.

Today is a great day to help mend the hearts of others.

Today is a great day to help reestablish the good reputation of another.

Today is a great day to seek the good in others.

Today is a great day to seek the goodness in ourselves.

Today is a great day to trust God from whom all blessings flow.

Today is a great day to see in others what they see in you.

Today is a great day to let justice prevail for one another.

Today is a great day to trust God and let the healing begin.

Today is a great day to be generous to others.

Today is a great day to help meet the needs of others.

Today is a great day to pray for one another.

Today is a great day to reach out to others.

Today is a great day to reach out and touch someone.

Today is another great day to keep hope alive.

Today is a great day to stand in your truth.

Today is a great day to do what we can to save the earth.

Today is a great day to dream big.

Today is a great day to realize this is your rainy day.

Today is a great day to recognize that God is good all the time.

Today is another great day to keep God number one in our lives.

Today is a great day to remember friends and loved ones.

Today is a great day to honor our veterans.

Today is a great day to pray for others as we pray for ourselves.

Today is a great day to wish well in the world, WWW.

Today is a great day to be proud of who you are and whose you are.

Today is a great day to end the hatred.

Today is a great day to stop the violence.

Today is a great day to be more loving, kind, considerate and humane in thoughts, words and deeds.

Today is another great day to focus on priorities.

Today is a great day to stop the violence and save humankind.

Today is a great day to end racism, ageism, sexism and save humankind.

Today is a great day to end the rhetoric and begin, again.

Today is a great day to be included as an ally.

Today is another great day to realize that everyone has worth.

Today is a great day to expect a miracle.

Today is a great day to ditch the rhetoric and let the work begin.

Today is a great day to share our stories with each other.

Today is a great day to seize the moment.

Today is a great day to greet others with Jesus joy.

Today is another great day to do your best.

Today is a great day to speak truth to power.

Today is a great day to give someone a hand up.

Today is a great day to soar like an eagle.

Today is a great day to have a wonderfully positive attitude.

Today is a great day to be hopeful and loving knowing The Lord is still in control.

Today is a great day to have skin in the game of life.

Today is a great day not to worry about things you do not control.

Today is a great day to have no regrets.

Today is a great day to recognize, safeguard and cherish life, liberty and the pursuit of happiness.

Today is a great day to reach across the pond.

Today is a great day to celebrate each other.

Today is a great day to seek social justice across our land and country.

Today is a great day to let the stripes we bear impact our commitment for change in the world.

Today is a great day to realize our commitment to change is too important to keep silent.

Today is a great day to realize change happens when we reach out to others by thoughts, words and deeds.

Today is a great day to wake up to joy, joy, joy, God's wonder working joy.

Today is a great day to be mighty thankful.

Today is a great day to be alive and well.

Today is a great day to recognize our democracy as a system of government of the people, by the people, and for the people, and everyone is equal and has a voice.

Today is a great day to celebrate our fathers.

Today is a great day being blessed and highly favored.

Today is a great day to reflect on the good in the world and keep it going and not perpetuate the evil.

Today is a great day to live, love, and laugh.

Today is a great day to take time for self-care and love to be full, fit and able to share with others.

Today is a great day to humble ourselves in the presence of the Lord.

Today is a great day to be caring, watchful and mindful of others.

Today is a great day to realize your journey is what you make it.

Today is a great day to realize if the waters are too rocky, get on a different ship.

Today is a great day to know that God is good all the time.

Today is another great day to remember in all things give praise unto the Lord.

Today is a great day to be the change that you want to see.

Today is a great day to praise the Lord for His grace and mercy.

Today is a great day to encourage yourself and others.

Today is another great day to exercise our freedoms in America of life, liberty and the pursuit of happiness.

Today is a great day to make a difference.

Today is a great day to tell someone how much you love them and show them how much you care.

Today is a great day to be a better person.

Today is another great day to serve The Lord.

Today is a great day to greet one another with Jesus joy.

Today is another great day to be like Jesus.

Today is a great day to be an inspiration to others.

Today is another great day to keep your mind on Jesus.

Today is a great day to remember who your friends are and make new ones.

Today is a great day to honor and reflect on those passed on and prepare with much prayer to move forward.

Today is a great day to let Jesus be the captain of your ship.

Today is another great day to let Jesus be the leader in your life.

Today is another great day to remember as praises go up, blessings come down.

Today is another great day in time, promise and opportunities.

Today is another great day to hold on to God's unchanging hands.

Today is another great da to be filled with God's goodness.

Today is another great day to be obedient to God.

Today is a great day to let your character, convictions and concerns shine through.

Today is a great day to shine through the darkness.

Today is a great day to fully understand God does not need us but we need Him.

Today is another great day to be kind to others.

Today is another great day to expect a blessing with your name on it.

Today is another great day to make time for those you hold most dear.

Today is another great day to feel the power of the Lord; see the beauty of His goodness; and appreciate the greatness of His tender mercies.

Today is another great day to love God, love yourself and love your neighbor.

Today is a great day to appear ordinary while tomorrow a champion.

Today is a great day to celebrate effortless perfection.

Today is a great day to realize God is still in the marvelous miracle making business.

Today is a great day to expect a miracle.

Today is another great day for a big win.

Today is another great day to be proud of who you are.

Today is another great day to respect your elders.

Today is another great day to be proud of who you are and whose you are.

Today is a great day to explore new horizons.

Today is another great day to realize the Lord allows ordinary people to do extraordinary things.

Today is a great day to be a champion of the Lord and spread the good news around the world.

Today is another great day to celebrate life.

Today is a great day to throw caution to the wind and be the best that we can be.

Today is a great day to remove the clutter from our lives.

Today is another great day to show some concern for others.

Today is a great day to reach across the pond.

Today is another great day to forgive others.

Today is another great day to forgive yourself.

Today is another great day to gird ourselves and face life's challenges.

Today is another great day to dig deep to win big.

Today is another great day to thank God from whom all blessings flow.

Today is another great day to tell someone how much you love them and show them how much you care.

Today is another great day to sing praises to The Lord for He is good.

Today is a great day to seek a closer walk with Him.

Today is another great day to be at one with nature.

Today is another great day to realize one can start all over again.

Today is a great day to not enable others in the depths of addiction but show care and concern along their journey to recovery.

Today is another great day to learn something new.

Today is a great day to expand your mind.

Today is a great day to expand your imagination.

Today is another great day to be there for others.

Today is another great day to give back to the community.

Today is another great day to be creative.

Today is another great day to be innovative.

Today is another great day to be thankful.

Today is another great day to be prayerful.

Today is a great day to take the road less traveled.

Today is another great day to give someone a chance.

Today is a great day to give someone a second chance.

Today is a great day to research all the angles to come to the right solution.

Today is a great day to survey the landscape and come to the right conclusions.

Today is another great day to put a plan in action.

Today is a great day to set boundaries.

Today is a great day to test boundaries.

Today is a great day to expand boundaries.

Today is another great day to be with the one you love.

Today is another great day to love, honor and cherish each other.

Today is another great day to relax and take it easy.

Today is another great day to surrender all to God for He is worthy.

Today is another great day to realize God deserves our praise and worship.

Today is another great day to remember to worship the LORD in all times.

Today is another great day above all things to honor our Lord and Savior Jesus Christ.

Today is another great day to let our Lord and Savior be first and foremost in our lives.

Today is another great day to realize JESUS loves me, this I know.

Today is another great day to know everything belongs to God.

Today is another great day to focus on God and His goodness and loving kindness.

Today is another great day to believe in God and His grace and mercy.

Today is another great day to thank God in all things.

Today is another great day to realize the will of The Lord is strong in my life.

Today is another great day to praise The Lord for He is worthy.

Today is another great day to sing like nobody's listening.

Today is another great day to look out for one another.

Today is a great day to dance like nobody's looking.

Today is a great day to speak your truth.

Today is a great day to face the music.

Today is another great day to take a spin around the park.

Today is another great day to let the grandchildren have their way with you, again.

Today is a great day to start the school year on a positive note.

Today is another great day to provide positive feedback to our children.

Today is another great day to boost our child's self-esteem.

Today is another great day to boost the self-esteem of our children.

Today is another great day to take care of your temple.

Today is a great day to seek refuge in time of danger.

Today is a great day to realize The Lord can keep us safe from all hurt, harm and danger.

Today is another great day to count your blessings.

Today is another great day to be thankful for what you've got.

Today is a great day to be thankful for the little things as well as the big things.

Today is another great day to be thankful for God waking you up this morning.

Today is another great day to thank God for allowing you to rest tonight.

Today is another great day to thank God for blessing you to see another sunrise.

Today is another great day to thank God for blessing you to see another sunset.

Today is another great day to praise God for speaking to your heart as the devil lingers near.

Today is another great day to realize God is wonderful.

Today is another great day to acknowledge that God is the Alpha and Omega, the beginning, and the end.

Today is another great day to realize what a mighty God we serve.

Today is another great day to try a little tenderness.

Today is another great day to share and share alike.

Today is another great day to remember in all things be true to yourself.

Today is a great day to realize the mind is a terrible thing to waste.

Today is a great day to live like there's no tomorrow.

Today is a great day to be rational in your thoughts; realistic in your goals; and relevant in your life.

Today is another great day to love, laugh and live.

Today is another great day to live out loud.

Today is a great day to master new skills.

Today is a great day to let things simmer and cook rather than boil over and burn.

Today is a great day to remember if every time we speak of war, we speak of peace, the conscious effort is there to change. If every time we speak of hate, we speak of love, the conscious effort is there to change. Humanity is worth the change.

Today is a great day to unwrap yourself for you are special.

Today is a great day to share with the world.

Today is another great day to acknowledge the mighty God we serve.

Today is another great day to realize God will part the waters in our lives.

Today is another great day to make someone as happy as they make you.

Today is another great day to let you know that I love you and there's not a thing you can do about it.

Today is another great day to realize clouds are only temporary with unexpected sunshine on the way.

Today is another great day to realize a pure eye allows the sunshine to filter through your life.

Today is another great day to understand God controls the universe.

Today is another great day to have the Lord order my steps.

Today is another great day for me to get ready, get ready, get ready for a miracle.

Today is another great day for me to realize I am a child of the most high God.

Today is another great day not to be overcome by darkness because God will bring the light.

Today is another great day to realize Jesus is the light of the world.

Today is another great day to realize forgiveness prompts new beginnings.

Today is another great day to know God is!

Today is another great day to realize God deserves our praise and worship.

Today is a great day to realize the words we share on FB can make an impact when uttered unto God, "Miss you every day and thankful for our connection."

Today is another great day to let go and let God.

Today is another great day above all things to honor our Lord and Savior Jesus Christ.

Today is another great day to realize The Lord will be with you always, even to the end of the world.

Today is another great day to realize The Lord will teach us His ways, and we will walk in His paths.

Today is another great day to remember the Sabbath day, to keep it holy.

Today is another great day to know Jesus saves.

Today is another great day to rejoice in the Lord always.

Today is another great day to surrender all to God for He is worthy.

Today is another great day to know everything belongs to God.

Today is another great day with blessed assurance that Jesus is mine.

Today is another great day to let our Lord and Savior Jesus Christ be first and foremost in our lives.

Today is another great day to worship the LORD in all times.

Today is another great day to realize God's got this.

Today is another great day to bask in the presence of The Lord.

Today is another great day to realize as long as I have Jesus, I have everything I need.

Today is another great day to be deliberate in worshiping The Lord.

Today is another great day to sing Hallelujah through your problems.

Today is another great day to understand it's not what you know but who you know, and I know Jesus.

Today is another great day to praise The Lord in season and out of season.

Today is another great day to acknowledge a women's right to choose. Did not say, honor, pay, accept, challenge, deliberate, deny nor debate, but acknowledge. And, when all the rapists are off the streets, then will we listen to an opinion.

Today is a great day to enjoy another lazy day of summer for in a little while, it will be over.

Today is a great day to put your priorities in order.

Today is a great day to realize if you can see it, you can be it.

Today is another great day to understand that color is value added.

Today is a great day to understand that while life may not be the party we hoped for, have fun along the way.

Today is a great day for you to understand that I may not shop for special occasions because every day is an occasion to shop.

Today is a great day to realize I cannot afford to be one dimensional, nor would I choose to be.

Today is a great day to realize I can because I do.

Today is a great day to understand that when you can see no further, use your imagination.

Today is a great day to understand when people are their foulest, show them up with kindness.

Today is a great day to use everything you want in describing yourself.

Today is a great day to realize that window-dressing is just that. . . .

Today is a great day to be calm in the storm and show others what you are made of.

Today is a great day to know if you fall for anything, nothing will pick you up.

Today is a great day to know you should never sell yourself short because others will do it for you.

Today is a great day to know tomorrow is another day to keep one foot in front of the other.

Today is a great day to understand when you dislike the path of others, choose a different path for yourself.

Today is another great day to realize you are your own person—take charge.

Today is another great day to keep color in your life—it's beautiful.

Today is a great day to understand if keeping a journal, keep it short, life is worth living.

Today is a great day to know when life hands you a curve just keep driving straight.

Today is another great day to make up your own mind about people and hope they do the same for you.

Today is another great day to dig deep, as far as the mind can go.

Today is a great day to go for broke. The pieces will come together.

Today is another great day to be kind because it matters.

Today is a great day to be prepared to be the person you want to be.

Today is a great day to realize hurt lasts for the moment and then it is over.

Today is a great day to understand you can fix things on the table if the table is large enough to accommodate others.

Today is a great day to realize life is a stage and everyone's a star, and only we know who we truly are.

Today is a great day to understand in dealing with people, know that they change.

Today is a great day to understand what's yours is mine and what's mine is mine and so, dear heart, we are even.

Today is another great day to understand life is not fair and don't expect it to be.

Today is a great day to know chaos is not a lifestyle I care to embrace.

Today is another great day to realize a journey begins with a single step. Let's hope it is in the right direction.

Today is another great day to enjoy the view along the road less traveled.

Today is another great day to realize life is like an ocean. Step in, the water is nice.

Today is a great day to understand everyone fits into my world and I could not live without them.

Today is another great day to stop swimming against the current when smooth sailing is the goal.

Today is another great day to realize good trouble is a full-time job.

Today is another great day in all that you do, be yourself.

Today is another great day to realize you cannot expect the best from the worst.

Today is a great day to realize a strong sense of self yields an even stronger sense of everybody else. Compassion and understanding are key.

Today is another great day to love the one you're with.

Today is another great day to be yet alive.

Today is another great day to serve The Lord in all times.

Today is another great day to sing praises to The Lord for He is worthy.

Today is another great day to thank a veteran for their service and share that we'll never forget the sacrifices they have made for us.

Today is a great day to bloom where you're planted.

Today is another great day to lift the name of the Lord throughout the land that we may be healed.

Today is another great day to trust the Lord that He will bring us together.

Today is another great day to be thankful unto the Lord for His goodness is everlasting.

Today is another great day to give thanks unto the Lord for His mercy endures forever.

Today is another great day to come together in prayer.

Today is another great day to realize it's your season to be blessed.

Today is another great day to know the Lord for yourself.

Today is a great day to expand our horizons.

Today is another great day to be intentional in praising God.

Today is a great day to help with inside chores.

Today is a great day to help with the task at hand.

Today is a great day to help with outside chores.

Today is another great day for fun, food and fellowship.

Today is another great day to remember Jesus is the reason for the season.

Today is a great day to give of your time, talent, and tithes.

Today is another great day for family, food and fun.

Today is another great day to realize how blessed and highly favored I am.

Today is another great day to have the spirit of forgiveness.

Today is a great day to throw your hat into the ring to represent others.

Today is another great day realizing that every day is a new day.

Today is another great day to know Jesus is the reason for the season.

Today is another great day to have your Christmas filled with love, hope, joy and peace.

Today is a great day to realize we can be a person of love and an instrument of peace and justice.

Today is another great day worshiping God and thanking Him for His tender mercy and many blessings.

Today is another great day to realize you can bend and not break.

Today is another great day to realize forgiveness prompts new beginnings.

Today is a great day to realize today is a new day. Make the best of it.

Today is a great day to plant the seeds for tomorrow's harvest.

Today is another great day to take the time to cultivate the mind.

Today is another great day to realize the only one standing in the way of you is you.

Today is a great day to end racism, antisemitism, ageism, and sexism and save humankind.

Today is another great day to realize the Lord knows every single hair on your head.

Today is a great day to know life does not end when you pass the baton. You pick up another and run on.

Today is a great day to remember for every dark cloud there is a silver lining.

Today is another great day to remember no matter how you dice, slice or serve it up, love matters.

Today is a great day to remember as love crowds throughout body, mind and spirit, there is no room to hate.

Today is another great day to realize as love permeates the soul, hate cannot abide.

Today is another great day to lift as we climb.

Today is another great day to realize this is our time. Make the best of it.

Today is another great day to know together we can do it.

Today is another great day to realize how much we have done, together.

Today is a great day to climb out from under the rock to see the light of day.

Today is another great day to realize the Lord works in mysterious ways in His wonders to perform.

Today is another great day to realize if it is heartwarming, it is heart rendering and out of that grow the seeds of love and compassion.

Today is another great day to know truth is the right option.

Today is another great day to understand anything bestowed is man-made, satisfaction comes from within.

Today is another great day to realize I need only to look up for my blessings.

Today is another great day to realize being yourself looks good on you.

Today is a great day to stop wasting time by procrastination. Live life to its fullest making every second count.

Today is another great day to live with purpose.

Today is another great day to let your life be a testament to the glory of God.

Today is a great day to be included as an ally for peace in the world.

Today is another great day to see yourself as others see you.

Today is a great day to realize for every action there is a reaction that could have dire consequences, or not.

Today is another great day to believe in yourself and the power in which the Lord has blessed you.

Today is another great day to inspire civic pride in the community.

Today is another great day to reflect on that which we are truly grateful.

Today is another great day to support your favorite programs to give back and provide new opportunities for others.

Today is another great day to remember the Lord blesses you so that you can be a blessing to someone else.

Today is another great day to be the best version of yourself.

Today is a great day to be kind to one another.

Today is a great day to realize God has smiled on you and blessed you to live and see another day.

Today is a great day to thank a mentor while you still can.

Today is another great day to thank your parents while you still can.

Today is another great day to thank the Lord for His grace and mercy.

Today is another great day to realize you are in charge of your own happiness.

Today is another great day to do the right thing and trust God when you do.

Today is another great day The Lord has given me, and I am thankful to be blessed.

Today is another great day to realize there are no wasted efforts because from them, we learn and grow.

Today is another great day to stop sowing seeds of discontent and resentment because it breeds distrust and anger.

Today is another great day to avoid being around negativity and insecurity because it destroys positivity and possibilities.

Today is a great day to be a plus, plus person to better enjoy a little something extra.

Today is a great day to spread a little joy and cheer.

Today is a great day to remember your happy place and smile.

Today is a great day to keep hope alive.

Today is another great day to realize positivity is like fuel for the soul and it can follow me anywhere.

Today is another great day to realize a good attitude you can take anywhere.

Today is another great day to love, care for and support our children making them priority one.

Today is another day to realize when we kill our own, it's genocide.

Today is another great day to pray, "Lord help us all".

Today is the day to take responsibility for what you do because others will hold you accountable.

Today is a great day to honor veterans who gave their lives in service to our country.

CPSIA information can be obtained
at www.ICGtesting.com
Printed in the USA
BVHW031952201222
654681BV00002B/2

9 798765 706916